How to Write a Report

BY GERALD NEWMAN

D0773376

A GROLIER COMPANY

A Language Skills Concise Guide
FRANKLIN WATTS
New York | London | Toronto | Sydney | 1980

For Mona
*who's always there to
help me do it right*

The author wishes to express his gratitude to the
following for their contributions or their assistance:

Marcie Rader   Theresa Lomonaco
Gary Portuesi   Danielle O'Hare
Joseph Aiello   Patrick Raziano
Holly Bartlett   Heather Sulzer
Gina Berg   Roseann Tsangaris
Peter Fiore   Eric Watson
Sara Longin

and to Aaron for his love and understanding

Library of Congress Cataloging in Publication Data

Newman, Gerald.
How to write a report.

(A Language skills concise guide)
Includes Index.
SUMMARY: Outlines ways to develop the research
and writing skills necessary for the production of
concise written reports.
1. Report writing—Juvenile literature. [1. Report writing] I. Title. II. Series: Language
skills concise guide.
PE1478.N4   808'.042   80–13017
ISBN 0–531–04135–2

Contents

The ink of the scholar is more sacred
than the blood of the martyr.
—*Mohammed*

Whatever we conceive well,
we express clearly.
—*Boileau*

Chapter I.
Why a Report?

As you continue your education, you will discover that most of your teachers will assign you one or more reports to write during the semester. This is your teachers' way of helping you to gain something from their courses in addition to the information presented to you in class. It is their way of encouraging you to go beyond the classroom for education. And it is also one of the best possible ways for you to become truly knowledgeable about one particular area of the curriculum.

There are valid reports to be written in every subject area. A history teacher may ask you to write about the causes or effects of an important historical event. An English instructor may require you to delve into the life of a particular author or to research some aspect of literature. A science teacher may want you to examine the life of a scientist to understand what motivated his or her contribution. Or you may be asked to investigate a particular chemical or biological process. Even in art you may be required to write a report, perhaps about some school of art or some specific artistic technique.

As you can see, writing a report is a skill you will need to develop and master for success in your school career.

At times, your task will seem difficult and frustrating. Writing frequently is. But once the work is done, you will have learned perhaps more than you expected. With each project completed, you will have improved in your ability to:

1. Choose an area for research
2. Limit that area to a specific topic
3. Use the library

4. Choose the proper books and periodicals for your research
5. Research a topic
6. Be selective in your reading
7. Prepare a bibliography
8. Take notes
9. Organize ideas
10. Create a proper outline
11. Write a first draft of a report
12. Use end notes
13. Revise a report

Most of all, you will feel a sense of accomplishment for a job well done.

THE ACCURACY OF REPORTING

The creating of fiction or poetry requires you to dig into your imagination and find or invent situations. But when you write a report, you are not permitted to use that same process. You are obligated to give the facts. This is not to say that you cannot find an interesting way to present the facts, or that, when called for, you cannot offer some opinion. It just means that whatever you put down on paper must be *accurate* and *informative*.

If your science teacher asks you to report about the moons that orbit Jupiter, you may certainly include information about Galileo's discoveries, Laplace's theories, and *Voyager II*'s photographs. But you would not give a detailed description of the *Voyager's* fuel or tracking system or Galileo's life as a child.

If your English teacher asks you to review a new biography of Muhammad Ali, you would undoubtedly discuss Ali's youth, his defiance of the law by refusing to serve in the military, and, of course, his fights. But you would not be permitted to describe your own wish to train for and become a heavyweight contender.

A good report contains accurate information about a particular subject. It is clearly written, easy to understand,

and to the point. Its purpose is to offer its readers what they want or need to know about a specific subject. As such, it neither omits important facts nor includes unnecessary information. Therefore, be sure that any topic you choose to write about:

1. Is interesting to you
2. Can be covered in a limited number of words
3. Can be researched
4. Can be found in various sources
5. Is worth the effort

Chapter II.
Choosing a Topic

Reports are usually assigned in one of three ways:

1. Students are permitted to write about anything at all.
2. Students choose one topic from a number of suggestions.
3. The entire class writes about the same subject.

The first assignment is the one least often given. But when it is asked for, its purpose is usually to provide your teacher with a way of judging your writing ability. Your teacher may be more interested here in your style than in your knowledge of the subject matter.

At first, the freedom of choice may be a little unnerving. What do you write about? Where do you begin?

You begin by examining your interests. You are always on firmer ground when you write about something you know.

Let's look at the second option. If you are told to select one topic out of many, be sure the one you choose interests you more than the others. For example, your English teacher may ask you to pick one of a number of novels and to discuss the author's feelings about a certain theme. Don't choose the shortest book just to save time. Read the book jackets or the introductions of a few of the suggested novels and choose the one you really think might interest *you*. If by chance you begin the book and lose interest in it, try another. Your grade will be determined by your ability to express the author's ideas. If you are not sure you understand them or if you are not enjoying the book, you probably won't devote your best efforts to writing the report.

Sometimes you may be forced to read a book you don't like because it's the only one that has the information you need. When that happens, it is wise to read quickly and with the sole aim of locating the desired material.

When the entire class is assigned the same topic, like it or not, you are in competition with your classmates. As objective as your teachers may try to be, it is impossible for them not to compare how the students tackle the assignment. Thus, you must find a way for your report to be unique. Your *approach* is the key.

Suppose the topic is *Dating.* The obvious approach is to discuss how teenagers date. A report comparing dating customs in another country with American customs may be a better idea. Or how about beginning with the story of how your parents or grandparents met? Times have changed and so having dating practices.

Suppose the topic is *Drug Addiction.* The obvious approach is to discuss the effects of marijuana, heroin, cocaine, or amphetamines on an individual, or to write about the laws concerning the selling of illegal drugs. Avoid the obvious. Instead, you might choose to write about the reliance of millions of average Americans on tranquilizers. Or you might even write about pain clinics that allow patients to use addictive narcotics legally.

LIMITING THE TOPIC

No matter which of the three assignments you are given, the subject of your report should not be overly broad or general. Limit your topic. Choose a *manageable* aspect of a broad area.

Let's assume your health-education teacher assigns a class report on the subject of *Disease.* You couldn't possibly write a report that included discussion of every disease.

Well, then, what are your choices? They may be:

1. Childhood diseases
2. A specific disease
3. How diseases are controlled or conquered
4. Immunization
5. A biography of a scientist who has found a cure for a specific disease
6. Physical therapy
7. The vitamin controversy

The list is nearly endless.

After you have completed a unit on American government in your history class, your teacher may ask you to write about one aspect of the U.S. Constitution. What topic might you choose? Consider these:

1. Why the Constitution was created
2. The First Constitutional Convention
3. Federalism
4. Separation of powers
5. Checks and balances
6. Adaptation of the Constitution
7. Any of the Amendments or Articles
8. Constitutional law

Even within these areas, there are opportunities to limit your research topic. For example, if you chose topic 4, *Separation of powers,* you could easily narrow your report to any of the following:

1. The reason for the separation of powers
2. The role of the Senate

3. The role of the House of Representatives
4. The role of the President
5. The role of the Vice-President
6. The role of the Supreme Court

And again, it is possible to narrow down *these* areas to even *more* specific topics. If you chose topic 6, *The role of the Supreme Court,* you might be interested in researching one of the following:

1. Trial procedures
2. Impeachment
3. Judicial review
4. Appointment of judges
5. A specific Supreme Court case

The idea is to find a topic limited enough so that your research can be thorough. A topic that is too broad will result in a long, rambling report.

Though you may have doubts about researching a narrow topic, in the long run you will find it is far easier to do this than to research a topic that is too broad. True, you will have to look harder for information. But you will be confining your research to just a few paragraphs from each source you locate rather than having to wade through pages and pages of unrelated data.

Chapter III.
Getting Started

Because it is a general introduction to nearly every subject, the encyclopedia is the usual starting place for research.

You may have an encyclopedia at home. If not, you can find one in your school or public library. Go directly to the last volume, marked *Index,* and look up the broad topic you have chosen or been assigned. Suppose that you are interested in one aspect of the Supreme Court. You look up "Supreme Court" in the *Index* to find what volumes contain articles on the subject. Then you read these articles. Even after you have read them, you will still not know everything there is to know about the Supreme Court, but at least you will have an idea of the possible topics available for a report.

Choose the topic that interests you the most and that will meet your teacher's requirements. You are then ready to begin your work.

THE WORKING BIBLIOGRAPHY

Different writers' manuals suggest different methods of keeping track of information sources. Some suggest you enter everything in a notebook. Others suggest using a looseleaf book. But perhaps the most common and effective way of recording sources is to use index cards. They are small, sturdy, and easy to handle, and are therefore recommended.

Each reference should be entered on an individual index card. In the sample below, the name of the encyclopedia, the year of publication, the title of the article, the volume number, the page numbers, and the author's name (as it appears in the article) have all been entered. The name of the encyclopedia has been underlined, but the title of the article has been placed within quotation marks. You may also want to jot down a few words to summarize the information you found.

The working bibliography contains all the references you have read in order to write your report. It is termed

---

C. Herman Pritchett
"Supreme Court," *Encyclopedia International* (1979), 17
386–391

"working" because it may not be the bibliography you include at the end of your report. Some of the sources you read will furnish useful information, others will not. However, until you decide which information you will definitely use, it is wise to keep a record of *every* reference you read.

Chapter IV.
Using the Library

An encyclopedia will not contain enough information for a complete report. It is meant to be only a general introduction to a subject. You will want to look further. Now is the time to become familiar with your school and public libraries. Be prepared to spend some afternoons there; researching is the most important part of writing a research report.

Most libraries have at least two sections that you will need to use—circulation and reference. In the first you will find books that may be borrowed and taken home. In the second you will find books that may be used for research and study but may not be removed from the library. These books are usually marked with the letter *R* for reference. You may take some of these books directly from the shelves. Others are in the stacks, an area closed to public access. The librarian at the Call Desk in the public library will send for the book once you have submitted a properly completed call slip.

Every book in every library is cataloged. Many libraries use a card catalog—a series of drawers containing index cards with the name of every book in the library and its author, as well as any additional information you may need.

Some libraries have card catalogs individually arranged by title, subject, and author. Other libraries combine all three into one card catalog. Still others have the information listed in bound volumes instead of on cards. Whatever the system, they all work essentially the same way.

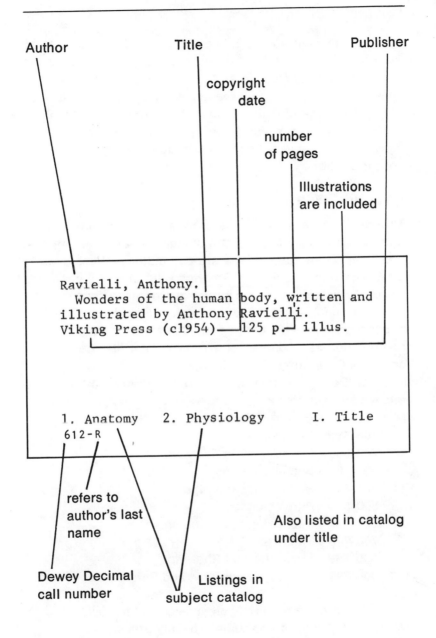

Author

Title

Publisher

copyright
date

number
of pages

Illustrations
are included

Ravielli, Anthony.
   Wonders of the human body, written and
illustrated by Anthony Ravielli.
Viking Press (c1954)——125 p.—illus.

1. Anatomy   2. Physiology   I. Title
612-R

refers to
author's last
name

Also listed in catalog
under title

Dewey Decimal
call number

Listings in
subject catalog

FINDING A BOOK

Suppose you want to find a book about medical discoveries. Pull out the card-catalog drawer marked *M*. Sift through the cards, which are arranged alphabetically, until you reach the ones that list books about medicine. You will notice a number on each card. This number is the *call number*. Each book, no matter in which library it is found, will have a call number, and that exact number will be on every copy of the book in the library.

CALL NUMBERS

The call-number system is a standardized arrangement of all subjects in the library. Each category is assigned its own code number or letter. There are two major systems used to classify library books in American libraries—the Dewey Decimal System and the Library of Congress System. The Dewey Decimal System is generally used in school and public libraries. The Library of Congress System can be found in federal, college, and professional libraries and in some public libraries.

The Dewey Decimal System divides books by numbers into ten subject areas:

000–099	General Works
100–199	Philosophy
200–299	Religion
300–399	Social sciences
400–499	Philology (Language)
500–599	Pure sciences
600–699	Technology (Applied sciences)
700–799	The Arts
800–899	Literature and Rhetoric
900–999	History, Geography, and Related disciplines

The Library of Congress System uses letters (except I, O, W, X, and Y) to divide books into twenty areas:

A   General works
B   Philosophy, Religion

C   History—Auxiliary sciences
D   Foreign History
E, F   American History
G   Geography, Anthropology
H   Social sciences
J   Political sciences
K   U.S. Law
L   Education
M   Music
N   Fine Arts
P   Language, Literature
Q   Science
R   Medicine
S   Agriculture
T   Technology
U   Military science
V   Naval science
Z   Bibliography, Library Science

In both systems, each area is further divided by letters or numbers to create an exact call number for every category under which a book may be included.

As you look through the cards on medicine, you will discover that the digits in the call numbers are similar on all books about medicine. If you go up to the shelves marked with these same numbers, you will find all the books about medicine that are presently available in that library. Take out several books at a time and skim them to see if they contain the information you need. Check the index and table of contents and note down the information as follows:

Author
Title (underlined)
City of publication and date
Pages you may use
A line or two about what information may be found

Once you have used these books, return them and take others. Before the day is over you will probably have an adequate working bibliography to be used for your research.

MAGAZINES AND NEWSPAPERS

The latest information about a subject may often be found not in a book but in a magazine. Suppose you were writing a report on the role of the President during a national crisis and you wanted to include Jimmy Carter's handling of the energy problem of July 1979. Chances are you will not find a book that offers such current information. But you could certainly find a magazine article on the subject.

Your public library will have a copy of the *Readers' Guide to Periodical Literature* in which you will find an index that lists magazine articles by author, subject, and title. You may then fill out a call slip and request a copy of the magazine. If the magazine has the information you require, be sure to make out a card for it. The notation should include the following information: author, the title of the article, the name of the magazine, its volume number, its date, and the page numbers. You may also want to jot down a few key words to help you remember the article.

> Goldman, Peter
> "To Lift A Nation's Spirit"
> *Newsweek,* XCIV (July 23, 1979), 20–26
> Carter determined to raise his own
> ratings by raising hopes for future.

If the magazine article did not list an author, the card would be filled out the same way, but the author's name would be omitted.

The latest and most complete information about a subject will probably appear in newspapers. But not every newspaper is kept on file in the library and not every newspaper has an index of its issues. However, *The New York Times* does publish an index that is available in many major libraries across the country. This index will tell you when and in which issues articles about your topic have appeared. The information should be recorded in the same manner as you would record a magazine article.

If your library does not have a copy of *The New York Times Index,* you may want to ask your librarian for an index of whatever newspapers your local library does keep on file. Another source of information may be the Sunday magazine sections of local newspapers, copies of which the library may also keep. Finally, you may want to stop into the office of your local newspaper and ask if it has an index of its own.

BIOGRAPHIES

Most biographical material will be found in the biography section of your library under the initial of the subject's last name, not the author's. For example, you will find the life story of Thomas A. Edison under *E.* Even though a subject's name may not appear in the title of the biography, the book will be found under his or her initial. A biography of Langston Hughes, for example, is found under "H"—even though its title is *Always Movin' On.*

Short biographies can be found in the reference sections in the *Dictionary of American Biography, Who's Who in America,* and *Who Was Who in America.* If the subject is not American, he or she will probably be listed in *Biography Index, Current Biography,* or *The International Who's Who.* These books also include biographies of Americans.

Chapter V.
Using Your Research

THE INFORMAL OUTLINE

While you are skimming references, you will be learning a little about your subject. With that smattering of information and your set of notations in hand, your next step is to compile an informal outline. At this time, you may not really know where your research will lead you, but with a simple outline you will, at least, know the direction.

At this point the style of your outline is not important. Listing a series of questions you hope to answer in your report is one way to begin your outline.

If you were reporting on the Warsaw Ghetto, for example, your question list might read like this:

1. What was the purpose of the ghetto?
2. What did the ghetto look like?
3. Who was forced to live in it?
4. What were the living conditions like?
5. How did people survive?
6. What was the Warsaw uprising?

These questions may then be turned into the topics you plan to cover:

1. Purpose of the ghetto
2. Appearance of the ghetto
3. Inhabitants of the ghetto
4. Conditions in the ghetto
5. Survival of the people
6. Uprising against Nazi oppression

With just this short outline as a guide, you can be selective in your reading and avoid any source that does not include material directly related to the above six statements. Your notes will be confined only to the information you need. But you can be sure, even as you restrict your research to this limited outline, that you will discover additional related information that will extend your knowledge of the subject and embellish the information you seek.

TAKING NOTES

From the initial reading you did to find your working bibliography, you should have formed a definite idea of what the exact topic of your report will be. That is, you should have narrowed down your subject to the particular aspect you will write about. It is now time to begin taking notes from the sources you have gathered.

There are a few methods writers use to take notes. Some use large yellow pads; some use looseleaf books or notebooks. But most use index cards. Not only are they convenient, but they can be arranged and rearranged until you have found the best organization for your material.

If you use this method of note taking for each reference you come across, you will soon find that you have a series of cards, divided into sections of information, or subtopics, ready for use. By using a different card for each subtopic, you will see how easy it is to organize your research.

As you read, jot down the information. Make sure, as in the samples given, that each subtopic has its own card and that each book used has *its* own card. For example if you find information on six different subtopics in the space of eight or nine pages of one book, use six different cards for that book—one card for each subtopic.

If more than one card is needed to record information from a source, be sure that the author's name, the title of the book, the pages, and the subtopic heading are written on each card. You may abbreviate when possible. Also, be sure each card in the group is numbered and that each set of cards is clipped together.

Suppose you are writing a report about the physical appearance of the Neanderthal Man. Your note cards might look something like those on page 17.

On the cards opposite, all the notes are in short phrases; sentences are not necessary. But sometimes just jotting down a few words or phrases will not give enough information. Therefore, you will need to write a few short sentences. Remember, you are not quoting an author. You are merely paraphrasing or reporting his or her ideas in your own words.

In one section of his excellent book, *Crime and Capital Punishment,* Robert H. Loeb, Jr., discusses the history of legislation concerning the death penalty in the United States. Note how one student condensed Mr. Loeb's information into a few sentences.

Death Penalty

Loeb, Robert H., Jr., *Crime and Capital Punishment,* 28–33

By the Civil War most states in the North and East had abolished the death penalty for most crimes. First to take the step was Pa., in 1794. It took more than 100 years, but by 1965 almost half the country had done it except as a punishment for murder and rape. Oddly enough, during that 100 years, 1 state reestablished it and 3 reabolished it.
1967–76—not one execution in America

Sometimes an author will say something so concisely that paraphrasing will not make what he or she has said any shorter or clearer. Therefore, you may want to quote the author. Be sure your quote is exact, including the punctuation. If you wish to omit any part, substitute ellipses (three or four periods) for the omitted portion.

Typical skull

History of the Primates, 161–163

Clark, W. E. Le Gros
skull—large, thick-walled
heavy brow ridges over eye sockets
forehead—sloping back
eye sockets, nasal cavity—large
upper jaw—protrudes
lower jaw—recedes
teeth—large
head tilts forward

Typical skull

Leroi-Gourhan, Andre   *Prehistoric Man*, 39–41
brain—not like modern man's, large
top of skull—low
face—similar to modern man though not as long
face size—larger

Bone structure

Men of the Earth, 107

Fazan, Brian M.
height—avg. 5 feet
forearm—short
walk—upright

Bone structure

Leroi-Gourhan, 41
legs—short
hands and feet—short, wide

Bone structure

Clark, 163–164
neck vertebrae—long
neck muscles—powerful
jaw—large
body closer to apeman than modern man

Mr. Loeb vividly describes a type of execution performed in Britain for over three hundred years. Some of that description has been entered on a card to be used *verbatim*—exactly as stated.

Drawing and Quartering

Loeb, 18.

"The condemned man was taken from prison, laid on a hurdle (a sled), and dragged to the gallows. First he was hanged, but not long enough to die. Then he was cut down and disemboweled by the executioner. His entrails were burned, his head cut off, and his body hacked into four quarters. . . . On occasion, the Queen [Elizabeth I] gave orders that victims should be conscious when the disembowelment began."

PLAGIARISM

You may use the exact words of an author, provided you give him or her credit. It is illegal—and unethical—for an author to claim as original that which another person has written. You are not even permitted to write anything that is similar in feeling or style to another person's work unless the original author has been cited. We will discuss proper crediting in Chapter VIII.

SOME ADDITIONAL POINTERS

1. Plan your schedule so that you can accomplish as much as possible in one session at the library.
2. Finish taking all the notes from an entire book or magazine before you leave the library. The reference may not be available the next day.
3. Review your notes to be sure they are clear, accurate, and complete so that you will understand them several days later.

4. Bring along enough cards, pens, pencils, erasers, etc., so that you can work without stopping to sharpen or borrow.

5. Work alone. Although it may seem easier to have a friend help you, in the long run it isn't. Your friend's notes may be confusing to you when you read them over. Furthermore, you may have to redo all the work your friend did to suit your particular needs or approach to the topic.

6. Know what you're going to do the following day. Before you leave, fill out the call slips or jot down the call numbers and titles of books you plan to pull from the shelves the next time you're at the library so that you will be ready to begin immediately when you return.

Following these few simple procedures will keep your work organized, and organization is the key to good note taking. You must always be aware of what information you have already recorded and what information still needs to be located. Each writer and researcher has his or her own technique, but those offered here are generally accepted as being the most efficient and effective.

Chapter VI.
Creating a
Formal Outline

CHOOSING A THEME

As you take your notes and follow your informal outline, one basic idea, the core of your report, will emerge. What is the essence of what you are saying? What is the main message of your report? Is it about the Warsaw Ghetto? Or is it really about the Nazi mistreatment of Jews who were forced to live in the Warsaw Ghetto during World War II? Is it about the Neanderthal Man? Or is it really about various archeological theories concerning this link in the evolutionary development of humans?

The answer to these questions will be the main idea, or theme, of your paper. That theme is the statement you will write at the top of the page under the word *Outline*. Later, it will probably appear somewhere in the beginning of your report. Keeping it in full view while you work, however, is a way to insure that no matter how many changes you make between your working outline and your final outline, you will still keep to that basic idea.

> THEME: During World War II, the Nazis forced German Jews to live in the Warsaw Ghetto.
> THEME: Archeologists disagree on the physical appearance of Neanderthal Man.

Once you have expressed the theme clearly and accurately, you can begin the outline. Your outline will be based, in effect, on the subtopic titles you have written at the top of your notation cards.

Arrange the cards by subtopic title so that you have several sets of cards in front of you. With your theme to dictate the order, choose the set of cards containing information that best introduces and supports your theme statement. Behind these cards place the next set of subtopic titles that logically follow the first set. Continue arranging the sets so that the subtopic titles of one set lead logically to the titles of the next.

After you have completed the arrangement, you should have the information in order and ready to form into an outline.

Remember, good report writing is based on order as well as accuracy. Once you state your theme, your information must clearly develop that theme in a logical, readable order.

THE FORMAL OUTLINE

Earlier, you read that your informal outline could be written in almost any form at all. It was meant only to help you keep track of your research. But the outline you now need follows a more traditional, rigid pattern. For this reason it is called the "formal outline."

Each major heading in the formal outline is preceded by a roman numeral. A subheading refers directly to the major heading; it is preceded by a capital letter. Each secondary subheading refers to the subhead before it; it is preceded by an arabic numeral. If it is necessary to use an additional subheading, that subheading is preceded by a lowercase letter. Here is an example.

THEME: Television's growing influence on our daily lives was begun with the editorial persuasiveness of Edward R. Murrow in the 1950s.

I. "See It Now"
   A. Premiered on Nov. 18, 1951
   B. Presented first live news documentary series
   C. Called "weapon of truth"
   D. Lasted seven years
   E. Presented with twenty awards in 1954
II. Murrow's programs of significance
   A. Showed picture of Atlantic and Pacific Ocean simultaneously on screen
   B. Explored equal education of blacks
   C. Revealed horror of Korean War
   D. Examined influx of refugees into Israel
   E. Enlightened public about McCarthyism
III. Murrow, the radio crusader
   A. Became pioneer of live news
      1. Showed Nazis in Austria
      2. Showed London during Blitz
   B. Show created anger
      1. Unnerved politicians
      2. Angered conservatives
      3. Called "constant stomachache" by CBS executives
IV. Show cancelled—1958
   A. Thought to be too controversial
   B. Led way for TV editorial power

A period follows each letter and number. If you are typing, indent each lesser heading two spaces past the greater heading. If you are writing your report by hand, indent each lesser heading about an inch (2.5 cm), much the same way you would indent for a new paragraph. Each entry begins with a capital letter.

Be sure all roman numerals, capital letters, arabic numerals, and lowercase letters line up one under the other, as in the outline above.

Because an outline is really the breaking of large statements into smaller ones, a heading may not have only one subhead following it. For example, an outline may not have a roman numeral *I* without a *II,* an *A* without a *B,* or a *1* without a *2.* If only one subhead is needed it should be eliminated by combining it into the heading above it.

Incorrect	*Correct*
A. Cats need protein in their diet. 1. 25–30 percent	A. Cats need 25–30 percent protein in their diet.

TYPES OF FORMAL OUTLINES

There are two types of formal outlines, the topic outline and the sentence outline.

The topic outline is a series of key phrases that lead from one idea to the next, each one derived from the phrase above it. The sentence outline follows the same order, except, instead of phrases, complete sentences are used. The two types are never mixed. Phrases may not be used in sentence outlines and sentences may not be used in topic outlines. A sample of each follows:

The Topic Outline
THEME: Though smokers know that cigarettes are dangerous to their health, many continue to smoke.

I. Oral satisfaction
   A. Babies born with ability to suck
      1. Associated with being held, fed
      2. Associated with warmth, security
   B. Children chew gum, bite nails, suck thumbs
   C. Adolescents and adults smoke, chew gum, bite nails
II. Influences
   A. Parents smoke
      1. Philadelphia survey of 96 students who smoke
         a. 40—both parents smoke
         b. 33—one parent smokes
         c. 23—neither parent smokes
      2. Portland study
         a. Boys imitating fathers who smoke
         b. Girls imitating mothers who smoke
      3. No pressure to stop from smoking parents
   B. Other influences
      1. Acceptance
      2. Curiosity
      3. Sense of maturity
      4. Rebellion
III. Nicotine
   A. Adults who smoked before awareness of dangers
   B. Various reasons
      1. Nervousness
      2. Habit
      3. Energy
      4. Weight loss
IV. Advertisements That Glamorize Smoking
   A. Romance, adventure, success
   B. Desires of young
V. Public Health Service and Surgeon General's Office Evidence
   A. 45 percent more colds
   B. Postsurgery complications
   C. Gum diseases
   D. Lung diseases
   E. Earlier death

The Sentence Outline

THEME: Though smokers know cigarettes are dangerous to their health, many continue to smoke.

I. Smoking is a form of oral satisfaction.
   A. Babies are born with automatic ability to suck.
      1. Sucking is associated with being held and fed.
      2. Sucking is associated with warmth and security.
   B. Children replace the bottle with chewing gum, nail biting, thumb sucking, etc.
   C. Adolescents and adults replace the bottle with cigarettes, though they often continue to chew gum and bite their nails.
   D. Thumb-sucking children are more likely than not to smoke when they become adults.

II. Young people are constantly under influences to smoke.
   A. Parents who smoke influence children.
      1. A survey by the American Cancer Society in Philadelphia of 96 teenagers who smoke produced these results:
         a. Of those surveyed, 40 had parents who smoked.
         b. 33 had one parent who smoked.
         c. 23 had no parent who smoked.
      2. A study in Portland noted that:
         a. Boys tend to imitate fathers who smoke.
         b. Girls tend to imitate mothers who smoke.
      3. Parents who smoke do not apply pressure on their children to stop smoking.
   B. There are other reasons why young people smoke.
      1. Teenagers feel they won't be accepted by their peers if they don't smoke.
      2. Teenagers smoke out of curiosity.
      3. Younger teenagers feel older when they smoke.
      4. Teenagers smoke to rebel against authority.

III. Adults rely on effects of nicotine.
   A. Many adults began smoking before the dangers were discovered.

B. Adults smoke for various reasons:
  1. Nervous smokers use cigarettes to hide anger, fear, or frustration.
  2. Habitual smokers don't realize they are smoking.
  3. Pep cravers think smoking gives them a lift, but nicotine is really a depressant.
  4. Dieters put cigarettes in their mouths instead of food to keep their weight down.
IV. Advertisements glamorize smoking.
  A. Ads connect smoking with romance, adventure, and success.
  B. Ads appeal to sexual desires of young adults.
V. The Public Health Service and the Surgeon General's Office have offered scientific evidence that smoking leads to disease and premature death.
  A. Smokers contract 45 percent more colds than nonsmokers.
  B. Smokers develop postsurgical complications more often than nonsmokers.
  C. Smokers develop more gum disease.
  D. Smokers develop more lung disease.
  E. Smokers die younger than nonsmokers.

Finally, if your theme is clearly stated in the opening paragraph and the entire paper leads to a logical conclusion, there is no need to label any paragraph "Introduction" or "Conclusion." A report is too short to demand an introduction or a conclusion. These two areas are reserved for books.

CHOOSING A TITLE

The title of your report is based on the theme. Choose a short phrase that summarizes your theme in a few important words. Based on the outline above, an appropriate title for that report might be one of these:

Smoking and Health
Why People Smoke
What Makes People Smoke
Dangers Don't Stop Smokers

The title of a report should always be written with upper-case and lowercase letters. It should *not* be underlined or placed between quotation marks, although a word or phrase within the title may be underlined or placed in quotes.

ADVANTAGES OF THE FORMAL OUTLINE

The formal outline offers many advantages. Here are just a few:

1. *It adds structure to your report.* You have spent many hours carefully researching your topic. If the report is haphazardly arranged and confusing to read, your efforts will have been wasted.

2. *It helps you stay on target.* The outline is a detailed plan to get you from your theme to your conclusion. Its structure keeps your ideas in logical order. Thus, when you have reached the concluding paragraph, the reader understands how and why you got there.

3. *It saves time.* You know from the start exactly what you want to say. You never have to stop to worry over what to say next. It's all there in front of you.

4. *It allows you to make changes.* Your note cards are complete and thorough. You have planned your report so that it follows a logical order. However, along the way you discover that something is wrong. It's far easier to correct an error in an outline than it is to rewrite the report itself.

Chapter VII.
The First Draft

You have been working hard for some time now on a specific subject. Your brain is jammed with more information than you think you will ever use—more than you've written on your note cards or put into your outline. By now you really know your subject. You haven't written a word of your report yet, but you've accomplished much. Feel good about it.

WRITING THE FIRST DRAFT

It is impossible to write a report perfectly the first time. No one, no matter how talented, can sit down and compose a literate, coherent piece of work, ready to be read, without having to make some revisions. You are no exception. You need a rough copy, a first draft.

The first draft allows you to get all your ideas on paper. It allows you to use the information in your notes in a logical order. It helps you to create clear transitions from one idea to the next. Finally, it allows you to see your weaknesses.

Prepare yourself for writing. Have enough paper and pencils or pens on hand so that you don't have to get up while you're working. Keep a dictionary and a thesaurus, or a book of synonyms and antonyms, handy.

And once you start, take your time. Rushing through the first draft just to get something on paper is often a time waster. The purpose of a first draft is to give you a foundation from which to work, but a weak foundation won't hold the weight of a well-written report. In short, work slowly and carefully.

Set a goal for yourself. You know how much time you have to work. Plan what you will do during a session and meet that limit—or surpass it. Don't plan so much work that you'll still be writing as the sun comes up. And don't plan so little that you'll be watching television within forty-five minutes. If you work toward a reasonable goal, you will accomplish more and waste much less time.

The first step in writing a first draft is to number all your file cards. Use a red pencil or pen and circle the card number so that it can be read easily. Once that is done, read the first set of cards, the set that pertains to roman numeral I in your outline. Use the information on the cards to draft a clear, strong opening paragraph.

If you are unable at the moment to write something really inspiring about roman numeral I, don't let it bother you. Though it may seem logical to begin at the beginning, logic doesn't always control creativity. There is no reason why the sections of your outline can't be handled out of order. Choose a pack of cards dealing with another part of the report, one you think you can manage easily, and do that section first.

Think of each section as a small report that will be combined into a larger one later. Each major part of your outline can be handled independently. Keep in mind, however, that each section must have its own beginning, middle, and end. Later, when you assemble the various sections in proper order, you may need to add transitions that will take the reader smoothly from one section to another.

As you finish using each card, write its number after the one or more paragraphs that contain its information. Read through what you have written to be sure that the words are your own, though the ideas may be those of another author. On occasion, your report will benefit from the exact words of an authority, either because the quote adds clarity to the topic or because it is said so well that paraphrasing will mar its value. When you find it necessary to take a direct quotation from one of your sources, be sure you quote it exactly as written. But it is not necessary to copy it from the card at this time. All you need do is to write "Card no. 12," "See card no. 12," or some phrase that will remind you to copy the card when you write the next draft.

As you use your note cards to write, keep in mind the basic rules of good composition. Each paragraph should consist of only one idea, expressed in a topic sentence that clearly explains what the paragraph is about. All other sentences in the paragraph should be clear and directly related to that sentence. More about the mechanics of writing will be discussed in Chapter IX.

CHECKING THE FIRST DRAFT

Once the first draft has been completed, take the rest of the day off. If you're not behind schedule, take the next day off too. Besides giving yourself a reward for working so hard, time away from your report will help you when you go back to it.

To properly edit a first draft, try to remove yourself from the work. Read it as if someone else had written it. You want to be as objective as possible while you consider the following:

- Does it analyze the theme?
- Does it follow the outline?
- Does it stick to the point?
- Does it say what you want it to say?
- Is it accurate?
- Do the sentences flow smoothly from one idea to the next?
- Do the paragraphs flow smoothly from one idea to the next?
- Is the topic sentence of each paragraph strong?
- Do the rest of the sentences explain and support the topic sentence?
- Does the conclusion work?
- Are the grammar, punctuation, and spelling correct?

If the answer to any of the above questions is no, now is the time to make corrections. Once you've done that, read the report over again so that you can honestly answer yes to all of the questions. Better still, give it to a qualified person to read. Don't be upset if he or she points out something wrong. Surely it's better to catch an error at this point than to have it appear on your final draft!

Chapter VIII.
The Final Draft

All the hard work is over. Your job now is simply to follow the mechanics of good report construction. Though the requirements relating to the format of a report may vary from teacher to teacher, the guidelines in this chapter are generally accepted as standard and are followed by students and authors alike.

THE HANDWRITTEN REPORT

If you write your report by hand, use 8½ inch × 11 inch (21.5 cm × 28 cm) wide-lined white composition or looseleaf paper. Reports written on narrow-lined paper are difficult to read. Write neatly and legibly, using only black or dark blue ink. Write on only one side of the paper. Be sure your i's are dotted and your t's are crossed, your capital letters are clearly capitals, and your periods are distinct. In short, make a good impression at the outset.

If your paper does not have a printed margin line, leave at least an inch (2.5 cm) margin on the left edge of the page and another inch on the right. If you can't fit a word on the end of a line, hyphenate it; don't squeeze it in. Do not force a one-syllable word into a small space at the end of a line. Leave the space blank and go on to the next line. For polysyllabic words, break them only according to accepted rules of syllabification. Check in a dictionary for how a particular polysyllabic word should be divided.

THE TYPED REPORT

If you type your report, use standard 8½ inch × 11 inch (21.5 cm × 28 cm) typing paper. Type on only one side of the paper, leaving at least an inch (2.5 cm) margin on all four edges. Be sure your typewriter has clean keys and your ribbon is fresh. If you make a typographical error, use correction paper or white-out liquid to remove it. Do not cross out or type over an error.

Except for certain quotations that will be discussed later, all typing is to be done double-spaced. Indent five spaces for the beginning of each paragraph.

CREDITING SOURCES

Whenever the words or ideas you have written are not your own, you are obligated to credit the source from which they came.

While you were writing your first draft, you copied your notes from the note cards. Along the way you may have discarded some of the notes you originally intended to use. Or, you may have added a few notes. If either of these is the case, reorganize your note cards using only those left in the pack. Renumber the cards and, as you write your final version, place the card number slightly above the line at the end of the last sentence you have copied from the card. For example, if you have included the following paragraph from your fifth card, it would appear in your report as:

> Rice enrichment has been practiced for years in some of the rice-producing countries. The International Rice Research Institute in the Philippines is working on the development of improved strains of rice and also on methods of enrichment.[5]

The number, in this case the 5, signifies that this statement is the fifth source you are using. It comes from your fifth note card.

If you are quoting verbatim and the information fills fewer than four lines, it is entered in the report exactly as above, except that you place quotation marks before and after the statement. The note card number follows it. Here is an example.

> . . . The Supreme Court has placed more emphasis on restricting the powers of Congress than it has on restricting the powers of the President. "Although the Constitution states that Congress has the right to *declare* war, the Court has never limited the President's right to *make* war." [1]

If the direct quote is longer than four lines, it is typed single-spaced and indented five spaces from the margin. If you are hand writing, it is indented about an inch (2.5. cm). No quotation marks are necessary, but the note card number still follows it.

> The first year of the Beatles and Beatlemania in America will always be the best years of my youth. I remember the fun they generated, the sense that something outside my world was happening. The Beatles were the one thing we all had in common—love them or hate them, you couldn't ignore them.[2]

LISTING END NOTES

Research reports, like everything else, change in style over the years. In general, the trend has been to make the process simpler for the writer, sometimes at the expense of the reader. Until a few years ago, credits were listed at the bottom of each page and called *footnotes.* It was a difficult process because the writer had to judge how much space to leave at the bottom of each page in order to fit in the credits. But now those credits are called *end notes,* and they are listed on a separate page following the text of the report. What has not changed, however, is the form in which they must be entered.

When you are crediting a book by a single author, the entry will be indented five spaces if you are typing, about an inch (2.5 cm) if you are writing by hand. It will contain the end note number, the author's name, and the title of the book. (In your report, titles should be underlined. Here, they will be shown as italics.) In parentheses will follow the city of publication, the publisher, and the date of publication. The final information will be the page cited. For exact style and punctuation, see the samples that follow.

Let us suppose you were crediting the book about the Supreme Court, from which you found the information given earlier. The end note entry would read:

[1] David F. Forte, *The Supreme Court* (New York: Franklin Watts, 1979), pp. 34–35.

The end note for the quote about the Beatles that appeared earlier in this chapter would be written this way:

[2] Ron Schaumburg, *Growing Up with the Beatles* (New York: Pyramid Books, 1976), p. 29.

Note that there is a space between the end note number and the author's name and that the word *pages* in the first example above was abbreviated as *pp.* When only one page is cited the abbreviation is *p.,* as in the second example above.

If a book has more than one author, the authors' names are all entered exactly as they appear on the title page of the book:

[3] Brandt Aymar and Edward Sagarin, *Laws and Trials That Created History: A Pictorial History* (New York: Crown Publishers, Inc., 1974), p. 135.

When quoting from an encyclopedia that has an alphabetical arrangement, the entry need not include the publisher or the volume and page number. Because no publisher is listed, the parentheses are dropped. In their place a comma is added before the date:

[4] C. Herman Pritchett, "Supreme Court," *Encyclopedia International,* 1979 ed.

If the author's name is not listed, the entry might look like this:

[5] "Lead Poisoning," *Encyclopedia of Health and the Human Body* (New York: Franklin Watts, 1977).

In both of these entries, the page number was omitted because the book uses an alphabetical arrangement. But the publisher was included in the second example because this encyclopedia is not generally found in most homes and libraries.

Government pamphlets, which generally do not credit an author, might be cited this way:

[6] Royal Danish Ministry of Foreign Affairs, *Jakobshavn, A Town in Greenland* (Copenhagen: 1977), p. 17.

Sometimes, instead of an author's name, an editor's name is given. In this case, the abbreviation *ed.* (or *eds.* for more than one) is placed after the editor's name and the reference is cited in the following manner:

[7] Milton Cross and David Ewen, eds., *Encyclopedia of the Great Composers and Their Music,* 2 vols. (New York: Doubleday and Co., 1962), p. 177.

Quotation Marks
and Underlining

Quotation marks are placed around the names of individual articles in reference books ("Lead Poisoning") and the names of short poems ("A Noiseless Patient Spider"), radio or television programs ("Happy Days"), song titles ("Yesterday"), short stories ("The Stolen White Elephant"), and magazine articles ("Sgt. Pepper Taught the Band to Play"). The complete entry for the magazine article just mentioned would appear as follows:

[8] Ed Zuckerman, "Sgt. Pepper Taught the Band to Play," *Rolling Stone,* 20 April 1978, pp. 50–53.

Titles of books (*The Abominable Snowcreature*), plays (*The Glass Menagerie*), movies (*The Wizard of Oz*), operas (*Madame Butterfly*), newspapers (*The Philadelphia Inquirer*), and magazines or periodicals (*Newsweek*) are underlined.

The general rule to follow is that if a work is a short piece or a part of something else, its name is placed between quotation marks. If something published is bound between its own covers, its name is underlined.

Repeating References

If you are citing a reference more than once, it is not necessary to repeat the entire entry as long as it is clear where the information came from. Usually, only the author's name and the pages used are given:

[9] Forte, pp. 51–52.

If you are using two books by the same author you need to include, aside from the author's name, the title or an abbreviated form of the title, so that the reader understands from which book your information has come. Suppose two of Robert Loeb, Jr.'s books, *Crime and Capital Punishment* and *Your Legal Rights as a Minor,* are used for a report. For it to be clear which Loeb book you are citing, the end notes of each book, *after* their initial entry, should read:

[10] Loeb, *Crime,* pp. 40–41.
[11] Loeb, *Legal Rights,* p. 24.

WRITING THE "NOTES" PAGE

Once you have written an end note for every statement that requires one, review your draft to see that all the end note numbers are in sequence. If a number has been accidentally omitted, include it and change all the numbers that follow.

Also be sure to change the omitted number or numbers on the index cards so that they will be in sequence when you write or type the final "Notes" page.

Begin with a first draft. List each source exactly in one of the ways shown in this chapter. Be sure that each source is listed fully only once and that the abbreviated form is used thereafter. Then be sure that all punctuation is correct. Finally, carefully recopy your corrected draft.

Let's look at a sample end note page from a report called "The Importance of B Vitamins." This page follows directly after the report.

The word *Notes* is centered approximately two inches (5 cm) down from the top of the page. It is written in uppercase and lowercase letters and is never underlined or enclosed in quotation marks. If you are typing, all listings are double-spaced.

Notes

[1] Morris Fishbein, *The Popular Medical Encyclopedia* (New York: Doubleday and Company, 1977), p. 112.

[2] Diana Clifford Kimber and Caroline E. Gray, *Textbook of Anatomy and Physiology* (New York: The Macmillan Company, 1952), p. 527.

[3] Fishbein, p. 113.

[4] Gerald Newman, ed., *The Encyclopedia of Health and the Human Body* (New York: Franklin Watts, 1977), p. 409.

[5] Alan E. Nourse, *Vitamins* (New York: Franklin Watts, 1977), pp. 77–79.

[6] Sarah R. Riedman, *Food for People* (New York: Abelard, 1976), p. 64.

[7] Kimber and Gray, p. 528.

[8] Riedman, p. 84.

BIBLIOGRAPHY

The final section of the report will be the bibliography, the page on which you list every reference you used to do your research. Be sure to include in the bibliography all references that have been noted in your end notes.

Skim through the bibliography cards you prepared when you began your research. Eliminate the ones you did not use in the final paper. Alphabetize the remaining cards by the last name of each author. In a bibliography, the author's last name appears first. If a reference does not credit an author, alphabetize it by the first word of its title, but disregard any *A, An,* or *The.*

If there happens to be more than one author with the same last name, the author whose first name initial comes first in the alphabet will be listed first. For example, Edwards, Henry, is listed before Edwards, Janice. Bregman, M. would appear before Bregman, Mona, because you do not know what the *M* stands for, and it is proper to assume that it may be *Mary,* not *Myron.*

Each entry is begun at the margin, but when the entry requires more than one line, each subsequent line is indented five spaces.

The punctuation in a bibliographic listing is a little different from an end note entry. Periods are used in place of commas following the author's name and the title of the work. Generally, no page numbers are provided for books.

A typical entry might look like this:

Trachtenberg, Marvin. *The Statue of Liberty.* New York: The Viking Press, 1976.

In certain reports it is possible to use many books by one author. In these cases it is not necessary to repeat the author's name. Instead, if you are typing use ten dashes followed by a period. If you are handwriting draw an inch-long (2.5 cm) line. The bibliographic entries would appear as follows:

Rosenberg, Jakob. *Great Draughtsmen from Pisanello to Picasso.* Cambridge: Harvard University Press, 1959.

————. *Rembrandt: Life and Work.* London: Phaidon Press, 1964.

————, Seymour Slive and E. H. Ter Kuile. *Dutch Art and Architecture: 1600–1800.* The Pelican History of Arts Series. London: Penguin Books, 1962.

In the last entry above, Rosenberg is one of three authors. The names of the other two authors appear in the order they are printed on the book's title page—first name, then last name.

Periodical entries are similar to book entries, except that the name of the article precedes the name of the publication and a comma follows the publication name and the date. The date of publication is also included and is entered as day, month, and year (26 July 1942). An article from a daily newspaper might appear as follows:

Knight, Michael. "Tourism Gripped by Fears About Gasoline." *The New York Times,* 27 July 1979, Sec 1, p. 1.

An article in a weekly periodical may appear as follows:

Haungs, Nancy. "Tap Dancing—The Next Step." *Soho Weekly News,* 6 July 1978, pp. 19–21.

If no author is cited, the entry might appear as:

"Carter at the Crossroads." *Time,* 23 July 1979, pp. 20–29.

As mentioned previously, a pamphlet published by a government agency often does not cite its author. Therefore, it might be listed in the bibliography as:

Royal Danish Ministry of Foreign Affairs. *Jakobshavn, A Town in Greenland.* Copenhagen, 1977.

The Bibliography Page

The bibliography is begun on a separate page and is always the last page of the report. The word *Bibliography* is centered approximately two inches (5 cm) down from the top of the page. It is written in uppercase and lowercase letters and is never underlined or enclosed in quotation marks. All listings are typed double-spaced. For "The Importance of B Vitamins," the bibliography page might look like this:

Bibliography

Fishbein, Morris. *The Popular Medical Encyclopedia.* New York: Doubleday and Company, 1977.

Kimber, Diana Clifford, and Caroline E. Gray. *Textbook of Anatomy and Physiology.* New York: The Macmillan Company, 1952.

Newman, Gerald, ed. *The Encyclopedia of Health and the Human Body.* New York: Franklin Watts, 1977.

Nourse, Alan E. *Vitamins.* New York: Franklin Watts, 1977.

Riedman, Sarah R. *Food for People.* New York: Abelard, 1976.

FINAL STEPS

Number all pages at the center top and place your name in the upper righthand corner so that if your pages become separated, your teacher can reassemble them easily. Staple or clip the pages together only at the top lefthand corner. Reports bound in book fashion are difficult to handle and difficult to correct.

After the report has been finished, cover it with a title page. In the center of the title page, type or write the title of the report. Don't use quotation marks, unnecessary capital letters, or underlining. Your name should be placed beneath the title and the date under that.

Chapter IX.
Other Types
of Reports

Not every report you write will be a research paper. Some reports will require you to do no library work at all. But most reports do require careful reading, understanding, and analysis of background material. And all reports require good writing technique. You may be assigned one of the following types of reports.

THE BOOK REPORT

A teacher may ask you to choose a book related to your classwork and write a report briefly discussing the information found in it. In effect, you will be reducing a vast amount of information down to a few hundred words. Here are some suggestions for book-report writing assignments.

First, and perhaps most important, read the entire book. You may think that skimming the book will be enough or that reading just a chapter or two will do. It won't. Reading only parts of the book will result in a superficial report, lacking in substance, depth, and insight.

Second, if you are not assigned a specific book, choose one whose subject truly interests you. If the subject is one you don't want to read about, your attitude toward the book will be affected, and your report will reflect your disinterest.

Third, if you are asked to read and report about a particular book, don't put it off until the last minute. That will only add pressures to an already unpleasant task if you don't like the book or the topic.

Finally, a book report may be written about any type of book—nonfiction, biography, or fiction. But no matter, a book report is just what its name implies. Don't attempt to retell the entire book. Find the central idea and discuss it as briefly as possible. The only details necessary are those that are important to the reader's understanding of the book.

A report about a work of fiction may include a statement of the book's theme, a summary of its plot, an analysis of its characters, and the reader's reactions. The sample below is a discussion of Christine Nostlinger's *Girl Missing.*

The love between sisters is stronger than family disagreements and misunderstandings. It is this love that sends twelve-year-old Erika Janda out to locate her fourteen-year-old sister, Ilse, who has run away from home.

Their background is a familiar one. Their parents were divorced when they were young. At first they lived with their father's parents. When their mother remarried, she took them to live with her and her new husband. Within a few years that marriage produced two children. In the meantime, their father had also remarried and had two children with his new wife. Erika and Ilse have one mother, one father, one stepfather, one stepmother, stepsisters and stepbrothers, and several sets of grandparents.

Even with such a big family, Ilse is very lonely. She is also very unhappy. She never accepts her stepfather, Kurt, and she hates her stepbrother and stepsister.

When she gets into trouble, Ilse tries to go to her real father, but he does not want her to live with him. The only one she is able to communicate with or trust is her sister Erika. When Ilse confides to Erika that she is planning to run away from home, Erika becomes frightened for her but is afraid to tell her mother. Ilse tells Erika that she is running away with her friend, Ann-Marie, to be a governess. Later, Erika is shocked to find that Ilse has lied to her.

To make matters worse, Ilse's running away causes her mother and stepfather to fight more, although it seems to bring Erika and Kurt closer together.

Several boys from school help Erika play detective and track down her sister. One of the boys, Ali Baba, really helps her uncover some important clues. It is Ali Baba who discovers that Ilse has run off to Italy with an older boy.

Erika's mother and stepfather eventually locate Ilse and bring her back home. But finding her causes more fighting and unhappiness for everyone in the family. In spite of this, Ilse's homecoming does do something positive. It teaches everyone a little more about themselves. Their mother learns that providing a place to live and food to eat is not the same as providing a home. Kurt learns that if he wants to have any effect on his stepdaughters, he has to assume some responsibility. Even Erika learns something: that her sister Ilse will continue to lie and might even leave home again, throwing the family back into a crisis.

Though *Girl Missing* is a sad story, parts of it are treated humorously. Erika's friends are strange and funny. Their humorous adventures make the story fast reading and enjoyable.

The author states the book's theme in the opening paragraph and follows with the situation or problem. Though the third paragraph does not truly grow out of the second, the diversion is necessary to let the reader know the background that forced the older sister to leave. The next four paragraphs summarize the plot and then the reader is told what the experience cost everyone in the family. Finally the author states her personal reaction to the book. It is a simple report, clearly written and to the point.

THE BOOK REVIEW

At some point, your teacher will undoubtedly want more than a book summary. You will probably be asked for a book review. The book review is a more involved piece of writing. It not only summarizes the plot, but it also discusses, and often criticizes, the author's technique.

In your book review, you may want to include answers to the following questions:

- Did you enjoy reading the book? Why or why not?
- Did the author provide the information you were seeking? (for nonfiction)
- Were you involved in the plot? (for fiction) If so, how was this accomplished? If not, why not?
- Did you like the author's style? Why or why not?
- Is there something special about this book?

The sample below is one student's book review of Stephen Rudley's nonfiction work, *The Abominable Snowcreature.*

> For about 150 years, people have claimed that snow creatures have roamed mountain areas throughout the world. But there has never been conclusive proof of their existence. I would have enjoyed finding some information in Stephen Rudley's book, *The Abominable Snowcreature,* that would finally prove or disprove their existence. Instead, Mr. Rudley relies on a variety of statements from people around the world who "say" they have witnessed such creatures.
>
> The bulk of Mr. Rudley's often-interesting investigation is secondhand information. But his work is thorough enough for the reader to retain interest in the many accounts of what the creature looked like and how it behaved.
>
> Because the descriptions vary from place to place, the accounts seem somehow less believable.

But that is unavoidable for, as Mr. Rudley points out, so many creatures, at first thought to be fictitious or nonexistent, have since been proven to actually exist. What has been described may, in fact, have been a number of different creatures, each unique to its part of the world.

Though some of the descriptions are interesting and some of the photography is fascinating, the photos often do not match the written words, so it becomes difficult to accept one as proof of the other.

Where Mr. Rudley's work falls short is in his lengthy discussions of the lands where the creatures have been seen and the people who have made claims of sightings. Some descriptions go on for so long that I lost interest at times.

Until a definite answer is available, I assume I must be satisfied with a book that gives only unprovable opinions. As such, however, *The Abominable Snowcreature* succeeds.

In the above review, the writer seems to be dissatisfied with what she found in the book. But notice that her criticism is offered with respect. She has not made rash accusations, nor has she made any statements she cannot prove through example. She has told us briefly what the book is about, but she has also discussed the style of the book. She has, in effect, satisfied most of the requirements of an acceptable book review.

THE POETRY ANALYSIS

Poetry is a special kind of writing. It is unlike all other forms of literature because rather than saying things literally, it chooses to use images—pictures—to help the reader "see" what the poet is saying.

Undoubtedly you will study a great deal of poetry during your school years and you will also often be asked to write analyses of particular poems.

The following guide may help you to organize your thoughts and make the job a little easier:

1. Include the poem if it is not too long.

2. Begin with a theme statement so that in one or two sentences you can explain the main idea of the poem. (What is the poem about? What is the poet saying?)

3. If possible, discuss the poem line by line or stanza by stanza, explaining the ideas or the images used.

4. If applicable, discuss the technical aspects of the poem, for example, the meter, the rhythm, and the rhyme scheme. How do these aspects aid the poet's ideas?

5. Conclude with how the poem affected you. Did you learn something new? Have you been enlightened about something you never thought about before? Have you "seen" something in a new or fresh way?

The poem analyzed below, "We Real Cool," is by Gwendolyn Brooks.*

We Real Cool

The Pool Players.
Seven at the Golden Shovel.

We real cool. We
Left school. We

Lurk late. We
Strike straight. We

Sing sin. We
Thin gin. We

Jazz June. We
Die soon.

The theme of this poem concerns the fate of the street kid in our society, a fate the poet believes is death. Brooks speaks through the voice of dropouts, teenagers who have left school and have replaced their formal education with street knowledge. They have become night people who terrorize others when they "lurk late." They go after what they want and claim it. They "strike straight."

Their music is jazz, not the music generally of the middle class. Their liquor is gin, which they dilute—"thin"—because they are poor. And in the heat of June, with their radios blasting, they hang out at the local pool hall, fully aware that they will die young because they have nothing to live for.

The poem's theme is strengthened by its style. Brooks uses rhyming couplets, a simple poetic form sometimes used in children's poems. In addition she uses only one-syllable words and incorrect grammar.

The structure, too, carries her ideas forward. It is fragmented. "We" begins each sentence, but it also appears at the end of every line—as if "We," in the last analysis, are the least important. Perhaps the speaker by the end of the poem has truly reached the end of his or her line: Note that there is no "We" at the end of the last couplet.

In the opening sentence, the writer of the analysis begins by stating what she believes is the poem's theme. She continues to elaborate her ideas by discussing the speaker's attitude, which she finds revealed in the lines of the poem. She concludes by showing the importance of the poem's form to its meaning. And though there is no concluding paragraph as such, the report has a definite, logical ending built into it.

THE STATISTICAL ANALYSIS

Many social studies classes investigate the use of surveys and how their results help to clarify uncertainties. Students learn how to collect facts, make observations, and draw possible conclusions. As a culmination, students are often asked to conduct surveys of their own and report their findings. Therefore, the statistical analysis is another type of report you should know how to write.

One student decided to observe pedestrians at an intersection in New York, in order to see how people generally react to traffic signals when they cross the street. The report that was turned in contained four major headings:

Purpose: Why the survey was conducted.
Procedure: How the survey was conducted.
Results: What the survey showed and an explanation.
Conclusion: Solution to the problem posed in the Purpose.

Red Light, Green Light

Purpose

The purpose of this study was to discover whether male or female pedestrians better observe traffic signals.

Procedure

Pedestrians were observed as they crossed the street at the intersection of Avenue X and East First Street in Brooklyn, New York. This intersection was observed during three thirty-minute sessions on December 19, 1978. The traffic light changed thirty times during each session.

Pedestrians were observed to see how many crossed the street with the light and how many crossed against the light. The observations were recorded in two categories for each session—male and female.

Results

Session 1, 1:30 P.M.–2:00 P.M.

Crossed with the light		Crossed against the light	
Male	*Female*	*Male*	*Female*
9	18	19	35

[two other sessions were recorded]

Totals for three sessions

Total pedestrians crossing the street

Male		*Female*	
108	+	109	= 217 pedestrians

Crossed with the light		Crossed against the light	
63		154	
Male	*Female*	*Male*	*Female*
24	39	84	70

The following graphs illustrate the observations for all three sessions.

Graph 1

A comparison of males and females who crossed with the light for each session.

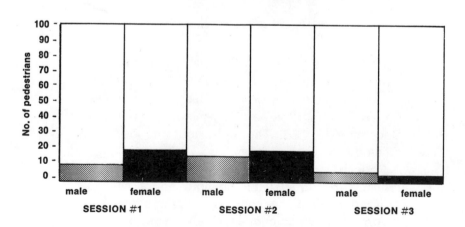

[two other graphs were included]

During the three half-hour sessions, a total of 217 persons crossed the street. Of that number, 109 were females and 108 were male.

During the 1:30 P.M.–2:00 P.M. session, most of the pedestrians were female (53 female, 28 male). Avenue X is a shopping area and most daytime shoppers in this middle-class residential community are female.

The 6:30 P.M.–7:00 P.M. observation period was the most active of the three. A total of 115 persons crossed the street (67 male, 48 female). The total is larger in this observation period because many people were returning home from work at that time, coming from the subway station, which is two blocks away.

It is interesting to note that during this period the greatest number of people (84) crossed the street against the light, probably because they were rushing home, and in their haste, they ignored the traffic signal.

Conclusion
Female pedestrians observe traffic signals more often than male pedestrians do.

You can see that the statistical report is supported by charts and/or graphs that pictorially clarify the collected data. Often, what would take many paragraphs to explain can be easily shown through the use of these charts or graphs. In the report above, bar graphs were used. But, depending upon the type of data collected, line graphs, pictographs, circle graphs, or any combination of these may be used.

THE REACTION REPORT

After having her class read a series of essays about the women's rights movement, one teacher asked her students to write a commentary on the position of women in today's society. She instructed the class to report their findings accurately, but because the topic lent itself to a point of view, a personal reaction would be acceptable. Such a report is usually known as the reaction report. It can also be referred to as the formal essay.

Below is one female student's personal reaction to male dominance in the English vocabulary.

The Man in the Moon Is a Woman

The English language discriminates against women. Open any dictionary to the word *man* and you will see how many prefixes are used to note masculine superiority. Open to either *female* or *woman* and you won't find one. But if you look at the spelling of the words you will discover that even these two words—words that should be our own—are not. They're derivatives of that other gender.

Let's begin with the word *man* itself. Webster defines *man* as "a human being." If only man is a human being, what are we women? Machines? Notice the last three letters of the word *human.* Even *human* is a sexist word.

Now let's look at *man-made,* meaning "produced by human effort rather than by natural forces or by animals; artificially or synthetically created." From this definition we are led to believe that women are not human beings. If man-made is human-made, then woman-made must suggest *inhuman-made.* There's just no escaping being insulted.

And what about the word *man-eating?* Are we not good enough to be eaten? If not, why are we always called *honey* or *sweetie-pie* or *cookie?*

The ultimate indignity is *menopause.* Men don't even have to go through it, and yet it bears their label (check the first three letters). *Menstruate* is another laugh.

How about *mandible?* If men say women talk so much, why do they get the prefix for a synonym of *jaws?* Or *man-of-war?* It's fine for men to label a ship as *she,* but when it comes to a vessel of real power, they name it after themselves.

Often we don't even rate credit for being killed. If my life were taken unintentionally, no one would record it as *womanslaughter.* Don't I deserve at least that much?

Our language is outdated. It is unfair to women and not representative of nature. From now on I'm going to say *woman in the moon, womanpower, womanufacture,* and *good womanners.* But I'll let that other gender have *mannequin;* that's a dummy.

Though the author has reported discrepancies in the accuracy of our language, she has also injected her own opinion into the report. Ordinarily, this type of personal reaction would be uncalled for. But in this case it adds satire and humor to the report and is certainly permissible.

Chapter X.
Writing Style

A report may be well researched, well documented, and well typed. But if it is not well written, much of the effort spent on it will have been wasted.

JOURNALISTIC WRITING

Perhaps the best way to develop writing discipline is to learn the journalistic style. Newspaper articles are tightly constructed and precise in their language. Imitating their style develops good habits that will be reflected in all your written work.

Look over your daily newspaper. You should readily see that there are many types of newspaper articles. But each one, no matter what type, is called a *story*.

The News Story

The most common news story is the straight news story, a factual report of a particularly newsworthy incident. The straight news story requires the reporter to relate only the facts as they appear to him or her without opinion or personal comment. The pronouns *I* or *me* never appear.

The lead, or opening, of a straight news story gives as much information as possible in the fewest number of words. At one time the lead was required to be in the first paragraph and contain what Rudyard Kipling called his six honest serving men—what, why, when, how, where, and who. But during the past few years, this "tight" lead has opened up to allow the reporter a little more freedom of expression. The pertinent facts (sometimes called the 5 Ws and an H) are still included in the beginning of the story, but these facts may now be spread over two or three paragraphs.

Journalistic style, in the lead or anywhere else in the story, utilizes relatively short sentences, short paragraphs, and pyramiding—beginning the story with the most important facts and adding less important information as the story continues. Pyramiding permits an editor to cut the piece at any point, depending on how much space can be allotted to it in the newspaper.

Consider the following lead. Note how all the important information is given right away. Of course additional information follows, but that information simply embellishes or clarifies what was already said.

Washington, Oct. 5—Secretary of Health, Education and Welfare, Joseph A. Califano, Jr., announced today that an all-out campaign has begun to rid the country of measles within four years.

The program, part of the National Childhood Immunization Project, would depend on the participation of local and state health agencies that would receive additional grants of 4 to 5 million dollars.

You can see from the excerpt above, that a well-written news story gives almost all of its information as briefly as possible at the outset. There is no real opening paragraph and, once completed, no real closing paragraph.

Another kind of news story, the feature story allows the reporter to mix facts with interpretation—to have a point of view. The feature story can illuminate the life of a celebrity, explain an unusual incident, or evaluate a government operation. It can treat the subject factually, humorously, or tragically, depending on the author and the situation. It does not need a lead nor is pyramiding necessary. But like the straight news story, the *I* or *me* or any reference to the author is omitted.

Though the feature story can be written in a variety of styles, each usually begins with an introductory or opening paragraph to gain the reader's attention. The organization that follows presents the subject clearly, using a more dramatic, personal approach than the news story.

The feature often includes anecdotes as well as facts. It is often more analytical, stressing the *why,* and is based on lengthy research, as opposed to the news story that, because of deadlines, must be researched and written quickly.

To show you how a news story develops, a sample is printed below in its entirety.

Sweet Dough Found
Behind Sourdough

Davis, N.H., Jan. 23—While shopping at a local supermarket, Sandra Storman discovered a wallet behind a box of sourdough crackers. The wallet contained $10,000.

Mrs. Storman, the mother of four, was shopping with her youngest son in Paces, a local supermarket. As she pushed the shopping cart past the display, Steven, age 4, pulled a package from the shelf. Mrs. Storman replaced the box. It was then she noticed the wallet.

"I was so annoyed at my kid," said Mrs. Storman. "I just told him to keep his arms down and then he goes and knocks down the box. As you can see, I'm very pregnant, so bending over was no fun."

Mrs. Storman still doesn't know if she can keep the money. But Sgt. Edwin Yabrow, of the Davis Police, informed her that if positive proof of ownership isn't presented at headquarters within thirty days, all the money will be hers.

"I'm not sure how I feel," said Mrs. Storman, when asked if she wanted the money. "If I lost all that money, I'd like to get it back. But now that the shoe's on the other foot, I hope no one claims it."

The five Ws and H were included in the opening two paragraphs so that the reader was told as much as possible at the beginning of the story. The paragraphs that follow relate details that lead up to the discovery and what the possible outcome may be. If the editor of the newspaper did not have enough room for the entire story as it was written and had to eliminate the last paragraph, the story would not include Mrs. Storman's feelings about the money. However, it would offer enough information to cover the incident thoroughly.

When writing a news story, remember to:

1. Report only the facts and not your personal opinion.
2. Include the five Ws at the beginning of the story, but not necessarily in the first paragraph.
3. Develop the story logically and concisely, expanding the information given in the opening paragraphs.
4. Pyramid the story.

CRITICISM

Each newspaper sets aside a special section for reviews of theatrical, film, television, artistic, and musical events or criticisms of books and restaurants.

Reviewers tell their readers what play or movie or television show had its first public performance the night before and what they thought of the production. They may offer an opinion about a book that was recently published.

A critic describes the standards used to measure a performance, work, or place, and then applies those standards with explanations and examples. The person doing the professional review or criticism must be qualified and must make an honest, unbiased judgment.

Let's look at the following review of a high school stage production. The review was written by a classmate of the performers.

The Ballad of Barbara Allen

When I walked into the auditorium, I noticed that the stage curtains were opened and the scenery was in full view. I was a little confused. There before me, in a black summer sky, was an enormous moon bathing a section of the Smoky Mountains in stark white light. Flanking the entire stage were enormous, lanky gray birch trees.

I had expected to see the stage curtains closed in the traditional manner. But this was not going to be a traditional evening. The unconventional beginning of the Drama Society's production of *Dark of the Moon* by Howard Richardson and William Burney created the atmosphere necessary for the unconventional play, staged by Mr. William Harris of the English Department.

As the auditorium echoed with the sounds of crickets and birdcalls, actors appeared—witches, mountain people—all the characters necessary to enact the tale of John, the Witch Boy, who yearns to become a human and marry Barbara Allen, the human girl he loves.

Witch Boy is told by Conjur Woman that he may have his wish only if Barbara Allen will remain faithful to him for one year. But just as the year ends, Barbara succumbs to Marvin Hudgens, her old boyfriend, and John must return to being a witch, destined to fly his eagle across the moonlit sky forever.

Especially in its mixture of music, dance, and folklore, *Dark of the Moon* fascinated me. Though somewhat sentimental in its writing, it nevertheless allows the members of the Drama Society to exhibit talents usually hidden in math and gym classes. Aaron Reilly was particularly appealing in his youthful energy as was Shelley Hart as the confused and tormented Barbara Allen. Roger Berman as Marvin Hudgens created enough tension and fear in the other characters to spread the feeling of discomfort right into the audience. The fervor of Fred Samson as Preacher Haggler, the minister who tries to convince Barbara that John is a witch, had us all handclapping during his church service.

In a small but important role, Peter Fryer was not only impressive as Floyd, Barbara's brother, but also as a singer and the composer of the entire score. It was unfortunate that the sound system made his voice sound a little fuzzy.

But the lack of clear sound was more than compensated for by Mr. Nigel's scenery, which floated on and off stage as if it were controlled by the witches' magic. Actually, it was managed by Harry Boyer's stage crew, which practically danced the scenery into place in full view of the audience.

For me, the most stirring moment came near the end of the play. Barbara and John are in each other's arms. The moon has risen and John must once more join his witch family. As he tells Barbara that she must die, she shouts, "I'm skeerd of dyin! Hold me John." Tears stream down her cheeks and down the cheeks of nearly everyone in the audience. It was a sensitive and emotional scene—a fitting climax to an effective production.

This student's effort, printed in its entirety, is an example of good reviewing. Though he was displeased with some of the writing and with the sound system, he concentrated his comments on the acting and the scenery, offering compliments where he felt they were due. Notice the adjectives used. Words like *wonderful, exciting,* and *glamorous* were avoided because they tend to weaken the effect of a critic's opinion. They can make a review sound more like a testimonial than an analysis. More precise adjectives and careful and thorough description allow the critic to show how much he or she enjoyed the play. There is no need to overwrite a review.

When writing criticism, be sure to:

1. Fully explain the medium being critiqued.
2. Be fair in your evaluation.
3. Avoid personal bias.
4. Be constructive and respectful.

THE EDITORIAL

Because a newspaper is not permitted to state its opinion in a straight news story, it reserves that right for its editorial page.

Stylistically, the editorial does not contain a lead, but it generally opens with a summary of events leading up to the stance it will take. Often, if the issue is clear, the editorial will dispense with an introduction and get right to the heart of the matter. However, it will always offer logical arguments based on known facts and experience and will avoid rude, slanderous, or undocumented statements.

Below is an editorial from *TV Guide* that discusses the Three Mile Island Nuclear Plant incident of March, 1979, not in terms of the possible dangers imposed, but in relation to television coverage of the matter.

As We See It

Three Mile Island. The name instantly evokes confusion. Management confusion. Government confusion. Confusion in the TV-news reports that tried to convey the situation to a deeply concerned people.

Accordingly, we call your attention to the article in this issue by Edwin Diamond and Leigh Passman in which they reconstruct what television reporters confronted as they sought to speed the facts to an anxious population.

As the towers of Three Mile Island loomed into the American consciousness, television—long since established as this country's primary source of news—found itself in what may have been its most difficult position. On the one hand, it bore the serious responsibility of informing the Nation, and particularly the nearby inhabitants of Pennsylvania, of whatever real dangers existed. On the other, it had also to remember its responsibility not to cause panic with alarmist news.

In the network newsrooms—with deadlines pressing steadily, with their reporters barred from the site, with statements from management and Government either not forthcoming or contradictory or questionable, and with the hydrogen bubble expanding hourly—the situation for the news managers must have been excruciating.

In the face of all these uncertainties—when the public expected certainty—one can wonder, not at the uneven performance by network news departments, but that they managed to do as well as they did.

We can only hope that both industry and Government have learned important lessons from Three Mile Island. But TV news, even as it struggled to discover a pattern of credibility in a mass of questions, doubts and waverings, did offer the Nation two conclusions: that we have much to learn about handling our nuclear-energy accidents and that we can never again afford to be unprepared to meet them.*

This editorial makes reference to a news story in *TV Guide* about television coverage of the Three Mile Island incident. But, like all properly written news stories, no opinions were offered. *TV Guide,* therefore, took the opportunity to state its opinion in its editorial.

An editorial does not report the facts unless absolutely necessary. Instead, it presents a point of view or a value judgment about the event.

When writing an editorial, be sure that:

1. The topic you choose is worthy of evaluation.
2. You do not retell the incident on which it is based unless it is necessary to do so.
3. Your opinions are well thought out and reasonable.

EFFECTIVE TECHNIQUES

Your ability to use language properly will improve your written work. The dictionary will help you to clarify the meaning of words and to spell the words correctly. A thesaurus will help you to find the exact word you are looking for. These books are indispensable aids and should be used when necessary.

But words *alone* are not enough to convey thoughts. Their combination in properly constructed sentences is vital to good writing.

More Effective Sentences

Do your best to avoid short, choppy sentences. Occasionally, short sentences may be appropriate. But when used one after another, they tend to interrupt the reading flow. Review your report and try to combine some of your simple sentences into longer sentences.

Less Acceptable

Wendy felt ill. She decided to remain home from school.

More Acceptable

Because Wendy felt ill, she decided to remain home from school.

Less Acceptable

Roseann wasn't hungry. Neither was Chris. They decided to hold off eating dinner. They would see a movie first.

More Acceptable

Because Roseann and Chris weren't hungry, they decided to see a movie first and eat dinner later.

Less Acceptable

The song was good. It had a strong melody. The lyrics were fresh and moving. It was a perfect song for Elliot's dramatic voice.

More Acceptable

The song was good. Its strong, catchy melody and fresh, moving lyrics made it perfect for Elliot's dramatic voice.

When it is properly constructed, the longer sentence offers the reader a single statement that is then supported by related ideas. It satisfies the reader's need to know as much as possible in one *complete* thought. On the other hand, if too much information is forced into one sentence, the reader can become confused and, as a result, lose interest. Consider the following two paragraphs. The first is long and rambling. The second attempts to repair the damage.

Less Acceptable

Each Sunday morning, Billy would put on his blue and white baseball uniform and without even eating breakfast, run down to the field, climb up into the bleachers, and watch all the men on the Middleberg Bullets warm up for the traditional Sunday afternoon game against the Wrightsville Tigers, the team from down the river that traveled up to Middleberg every Sunday just to try to beat the Bullets but never succeeded because of their weak pitching.

More Acceptable

Each Sunday morning, Billy would put on his blue and white baseball uniform. Without even eating breakfast, he would run down to the field and watch the Middleberg Bullets warm up. He would climb up into the bleachers and watch the men get ready for the traditional Sunday afternoon game against the Wrightsville Tigers. The Tigers would come up the river from Wrightsville every Sunday, ready to beat Middleberg. But they never did. No matter how hard they played, their pitching was always too weak to keep the Bullets from winning.

Below are two versions of paragraphs from a book report about Langston Hughes. Notice how the student combined the short sentences in the first version into longer, more interesting sentences for her final copy.

Less Acceptable

Langston's mother tried to register Langston at the nearest school. The nearest school was classified as "white." The authorities asked Mrs. Hughes to register him at the nearest "black" school. She refused. She took her case to the Topeka School Board and won.

Langston attended the Harrison Street School. There he encountered prejudice for the first time. He was intelligent and curious. He couldn't understand why suddenly stones were being thrown at him. He didn't know why the children were chasing him. And he didn't know why remarks were being made about him, even by his teachers.

More Acceptable

Langston's mother tried to register Langston at the nearest school. But because that school was classified as "white," the authorities asked Mrs. Hughes to register him at the nearest "black" school. She refused, took her case to the Topeka School Board, and won.

When Langston attended the Harrison Street School, he encountered prejudice for the first time. An intelligent and curious boy, he couldn't understand why suddenly stones were being thrown at him, children were chasing him home, and remarks were being made about him, even by his teachers.

More Effective
Paragraphs

A paragraph is a series of sentences containing one basic idea. Its spine is the topic sentence, around which all the other sentences revolve.

Each sentence in a paragraph should support a topic sentence. As you review your first draft, check to see that each paragraph has an effective topic sentence. To avoid monotony, do not place the topic sentence in the same place in each paragraph. Vary its position by using it as an opening sentence, in the middle of the paragraph, or as a closing sentence—depending on where you want the emphasis. Consider these three paragraphs:

It has not yet been determined how many minerals a cat's body needs for maintaining good health. Though tests have been performed, veterinarians still assume cats need only as many vitamins as humans or dogs. One important test allowed a cat to eat uncooked meat and cooked hearts (which have few minerals). After seven days the cat was uncoordinated, unstable, and nervous. Its bones were weak and its liver showed signs of damage. When the diet was changed to include foods high in calcium, iodine, and other important minerals, the cat's health returned.

Fat in a cat's diet is beneficial to its fur and skin. If your cat's diet has an insufficient amount of fat, add about four tablespoons of bacon fat, cooking oil, or butter to its food. *The diet should be thirty-five to forty percent fat.*

Some cats are nibblers. Some have one meal per day, while others have two. If your cat is a finicky eater, offer him or her food at the normal mealtime. If he or she refuses it, offer it again fifteen minutes later. Eventually, the cat will eat, because *all normal cats will eat almost anything, if they are hungry.* If, after a few days, your cat still doesn't eat, bring it to your vet for a checkup.

In the first paragraph the topic sentence drew the reader into the paragraph. A statement was made and additional information was included to support the topic sentence. In the second paragraph, the topic sentence was the conclusion to the paragraph. In the third, introductory details were given that led to the topic sentence. Then, to back up the topic sentence, more information was added.

Transitions
Though each paragraph contains information about only one idea, there nevertheless must be a transition from one para-

graph to the next. Some transitional words or phrases commonly used at the beginning of paragraphs are:

Example: For example, For instance, As an illustration, In fact,

Comparison: By way of comparison, Similarly,

Contrast: But, However, On the other hand, Otherwise, Nevertheless, Yet, In spite of, On the contrary,

Summary: As a result, In short, To summarize, In conclusion, On the whole,

Result: Because, Since, Therefore, Then,

Time: Meanwhile, Then, At last, Until, Afterward,

Ideas as well as words are used to form transitions between paragraphs. In the paragraphs below, note how easily the author moves from one idea to the next.

> Cigarette advertisements have been successful in glamorizing smoking. They connect smoking with the pleasures of outdoor life, romance, adventure, and success. In particular, they appeal to the desires of young men and women.
>
> Because of this appeal, radio and television are no longer permitted to show cigarette commercials. The Federal Communications Commission instituted the ban as a measure of public safety. But there are no restrictions on printed advertisements, which continue to show young, handsome people with cigarettes in their mouths.

There is a clearly identified transition from one paragraph to the next in the excerpt above. The first paragraph discusses the general influence of cigarette advertisements, while the second specifically discusses radio and television ads. The word *appeal,* which appears at the end of the first paragraph and the beginning of the second, serves as a transition between them.

Originality

Finally, grab the reader's attention. Make your writing sparkle. Try for the unusual. Attempt to convey your thoughts in an original way, as this student has in the opening of her report about Dwight D. Eisenhower:

> The fifties. It was the decade of fear: the building of bomb shelters, the threat of communism swallowing the world, the invasion of South Korea, the firing of General MacArthur, the humiliation of J. Robert Oppenheimer, the witchhunts of Senator Joe McCarthy. And amid these fears—or perhaps because of them—America elected its distinguished World War II general, Dwight David Eisenhower, as President of the United States, by a record-breaking 33 million votes.
>
> The catch phrase "I Like Ike" swept the nation. Even Adlai Stevenson, Eisenhower's Democratic opponent, was once quoted as saying, "I like Ike too." Obviously, he didn't like him well enough to vote for him. But the public did. It believed a button developed by a public relations firm that read: "Ike and Dick—Sure to click." The Dick was Richard M. Nixon, Ike's Vice-President.

ACCEPTING CRITICISM

Like painting or playing a musical instrument, writing is a talent. And like any talent, it needs to be guided and perfected.

As you continue your education, your teachers will help you to develop your writing skills. Each will have a different approach toward teaching you how to improve your writing ability. Learn from all of them. Take full advantage of their talent and their experience.

Most of all, don't be offended by criticism. Welcome it. Authors sometimes see what they *think* they have written, not what they have *actually* written. Let your teachers, who are qualified judges of your ability, tell you where your work needs strengthening, and follow their suggestions. There is always room for improvement. But unless you keep writing—and re-writing—you cannot and will not improve.

Index